CURRENT MOOD:

STAYING READY TO SUCCEED

ROD SHIPP

LULU PRESS, INC.

CURRENT MOOD:

STAYING READY TO

SUCCEED

ROD SHIPP

Published in Memphis, Tennessee by Rodricus Shipp.

Publication made possible by Lulu Press, Inc.

Printed in the United States of America.

ISBN 978-1-365-96824-2 (hard cover)
Imprint: Lulu.com

This book is dedicated to my guy **Wesley Maclin**. If anyone was always ready to get up and get out and make a move to become different and better it was Wes! I love you man and there will NEVER be another soul on this earth like yours homie!

Table of Contents

Preface

Hi everyone. I pray that all is well with each and every one of you and I would like to extend my thanks to you in obtaining a copy of this book. Life as many may know can be full of twists and turns which makes it hard to understand who we really are supposed to be and how we are supposed to live. In my opinion, I believe that everyone is supposed to be successful at something but determining what that "something" is has been the task for many people. We all experience life differently and encounter many unexpected paths along the way but I'm a firm believer that your purpose in life will continue to smack you in the face in some shape, form, or fashion and it's up to you to be open enough to recognize it one day and run with it. In most cases we see it and aren't ready to pursue. Then there are some situations where we see it and are afraid to dive in from fear of failure, fear of what people may say or think, or fear of the uncertainty of what to fully expect. In other situations we see it, but we are simply stuck doing what we think we are supposed to be doing and miss out on what could have been a blessing for our life. Whatever the case may be, I hope that this book helps you find what's inside of you to elevate you to the next level in your life so that you can truly fulfill your dreams, generate amazing peace, and encounter massive happiness as a result. I pray you enjoy the read and God bless you again.

CHAPTER 1

WHERE DO WE START

I remember when I was in high school, I had my mind made up that I would be a dentist. I was in the health sciences program that was offered at my school and competed in the dentistry sections of the district and regional competitions that would be held each year against other schools around the state and country. I was all in with the idea that when I graduated, I would find a top notch dentistry program and study my way into having my own practice one day. Then the day came that every high school senior lives for (so they can miss class)...college campus visits! Up until that point I had it mapped out, so I was really just looking to have a free day. I went on each visit with zero expectation and could care less what each school wanted to show us as they creatively tried to persuade these seventeen and eighteen year old's why their college would be the best decision we ever made. Needless to say, several things at each school that was presented sounded great! Beforehand, I hadn't even attempted to consider anything else outside of dentistry. But I also never had a well laid out plan of different professions and courses placed in front of me either so when I finally got to compare and contrast many different opportunities, my brain woke up and considered everything as a potential option. So now what? That's the question that I had to present myself with and up until that time, I had never considered that anything needed to be questioned. I would go to a good school with an amazing dental program, run track, graduate, and work my way up to becoming a dental hygienist full time. Now I have no clue if this is what I really want and if the school I had mentally selected was even the right choice anymore. For most of us, the confusion of life starts at that time. You are in school filling out all these applications for college and forced to pick a career when you barely know what a tax form looks like. And then that same pattern continues for another four to six years or decades for a great majority still trying to figure where they are supposed to be in life after thirty.

Sometimes it's not the career or employment path that's in question. It could be the "how" that floods your thoughts. What do I mean by that you ask? You may know exactly what you want to do but have no idea in what capacity. Well, Rod, I would like to teach but I don't really like dealing with small children or smart mouthed teenagers. I would like to help people in the hospital but can't get over seeing blood or needing to help "change" someone. I really want to encourage people but have a fear of public speaking. These are some examples of what it looks like to have a desire to be in a particular area but not sure how you can contribute to those things as you have preferences that you aren't willing to bypass. What's amazing is we live in a world today where practically NOTHING is impossible! People are making a living doing things that twenty years ago would have gotten you checked into a psych ward! Now nothing seems farfetched or taboo anymore and basically anything you want to create may be acceptable enough for the right people that allows you to make a living doing what you enjoy. The question is what do you enjoy?

I used to believe that we had to do what we had to do and that's just the way it is. You go years hearing and seeing the many men and women in your life expressing how this is the way things are and you can't always do what you want, but sometimes you must simply do what you can to survive. Now, don't get it twisted. Do I think this is the case for everyone? Absolutely not! By no means am I implying that everyone gets a fair shot. But I do believe that we all can make choices and decisions even in the positions that we are in to get closer and closer to where we really want to be. The problem with this situation isn't a matter of what is possible for you to do. The bottom line, are you willing to get uncomfortable doing things you really have no desire doing until you get where you want to be? In every situation there is always a way out. Some are more clearer than others but many times we are faced with the task of applying ourselves to certain activities, goals, or standards that go against our level of comfort, but when done accordingly can very well place us in those ideal positions that we have longed for. An example of this is very prevalent in sports. You have sports figures that will go on record to say that certain individuals would work-out while others were sleeping, partying, lounging, and anything else unproductive to the sport. As a result, those guys and young ladies would be at the top of the rankings more consistently than others. If they could have achieved the same results by sleeping longer, spending time with friends and family more often, or watching tv, I'm sure they would have taken those options? In fact,

I'm almost certain most of them would have. But they were willing to uncomfortably give up sleep, lose television time, eat certain foods and not their favorite dishes, dismiss time partying, and miss out on many life events in order to get closer to the position that they wanted. The same can be said of career choices or passions. Yes, you hate the position that you currently have on your job meanwhile when you are off work you spend no time participating in online seminars or physically attending workshops that teach more about the craft that interests you because you are too tired or find something unimportant that's makes you "too busy" to attend. Who's not to say that the one weekend you were off work and attended a function that someone there, who may be very important, noticed you and offered you a deal to do what you love. Or to take it a step further what if you decided to go to a function of some sort and meet someone who, after sharing a small conversation with you, decided to give you the very nuggets you needed to get your own platform off the ground and tips that could free you from your unwanted job. (Shrugs shoulders) I'm just saying. At some point we have to be willing to assassinate the excuses and destroy the debilitating thoughts that continue to stagnate our progression in life which we will talk more about in chapter five.

So you may be asking the question, "what gives you the right to tell us how to find what we may enjoy in life and make a career out of it. Like we've never heard of you so you can't be too important!" Well said and you are very much correct in your observation. You have no idea who I am and why I would even qualify myself to be credible enough to share any information at all about success. So let me start by sharing a few things with you so that you can know that I'm not simply throwing words together but actively, as we speak, creating my very own narrative in life that after a few years of trial and error, sleepless nights working my body pass its limitations, missing out on life activities and events with friends and family, and risking it all experiencing uncompromising discomfort while doing it, I can now say that I am truly enjoying life and nothing that I do to make an income feels like work. I found a way to completely do the very thing I love to do, which is helping and serving people, in a capacity that many wouldn't view as lucrative yet I'm able to enjoy travel, investing, and many other things simply from taking a season to sacrifice everything that makes us comfortable in order to get the results I have today. My results are NOT typical as it takes a lot of personal development and discipline to program yourself to do more of what you ABSOLUTELY don't want to do in order to be able to one day obtain the very best life you desire to have. And do not be misconstrued by what it means to have the "best life". Many people seem to think that term only applies to being rich and wealthy financially and that's not everyone's end all. I by no means consider myself rich or wealthy from a financial standpoint. But when I think of the term my "best life" it looks like what I experience now. I cannot tell you the last time I felt stress of any kind…at all. I literally have no desire to do anything differently than I do currently and when I decide to work it's on my own schedule, which we will discuss the importance of a schedule in a later chapter, that I strategically create based on things I prefer to do. So when people see me doing anything please believe it's something I actually wanted to do. I currently participate in the transportation and food delivery industry which I am grateful to say I started with and currently involve what many consider "gig apps" but has led me to be my own boss, help others, travel the world, and create my own business from the connections I've made with different people from all over. I work-out consistently, treat myself to nice restaurants weekly (yes I placed those two sentences next to each other), and spend time reading books that build me spiritually. I would like at this time to rebuke an earlier statement that I made. In reference to health and sanity I am very much what we can consider wealthy. I am rich in laughter and smiles and make time to remember my past years often as a reminder that life can truly be what you choose if you are willing to make the sacrifices and commit to your growth mentally, spiritually, and emotionally. Everything else important will follow. So take time to visualize where you want to be and see yourself doing EXACTLY what it is that you want to do and never lose sight of that. Eventually what you spend so much time seeing mentally becomes the very thing you can see physically. But it starts with the decision that nothing will stop you from being YOU!

CHAPTER 2

POWER IN YOUR WORDS

One of the most mentioned bible verses, which I'm sure you've heard several times in your lifetime, says 'as a man thinketh so is he'. And I feel there is nothing truer than that statement alone. Regardless how you may feel about that or the level of belief you have about this verse, there is one thing that is a certain fact…we are exactly what we say we are! Look back on all the times you verbally confessed something big or small. How many times did you say, "Oh, I can't do that." Or maybe you said, "Yeah, that's not for somebody like me." If those don't sound familiar what about, "They're probably gonna give that position to somebody they know." Think about how many times God had something lined up for you but then you used your gift against yourself. Don't believe me? When was the last time you spoke against being able to have something and still got it the way you wanted it? Happens very rarely, huh? Like once every ten times maybe, give or take? "I'm never gonna get the money in time to pay this bill!" "There is no way a woman like that would marry a man like me!" "I don't know why I keep applying for this position because they aren't going to ever give it to me!" We repeatedly use our own words against ourselves over and over and over and then dig a deep ditch to have a pity party because nothing is going our way, but really, on second thought, everything really is going the way we "call it". For years, I have wondered why and when we as a people adapted the practice of self-sabotage when it came to creating things verbally for ourselves. One of the most profound books that I have ever read was "Think and Grow Rich" by Napoleon Hill. I highly recommend this book for those who want to completely change the way they think and speak in terms of creating success and happiness for their life. Majority of the things and positions that I have or had in my life I didn't qualify for, particularly earn, or was even originally considered for such. The one common denominator that remains a factor in my life today is that I intentionally speak on the very things that I want and I believe that they are already mine mentally. In chapter six I will discuss more on what I mean when I say be intentional with your words. For now, what I will say is that you have more power than you will ever know. If you study many of the world's most successful businessmen, athletes, inventors, and entrepreneurs they will all have a similar answer when asked how did they know that they would succeed. Almost more times than not they will mention how they visualized themselves already in the position they wanted to be in or they spoke the very things they wanted until it became something they could physically touch.

What I'm about to say is not a guarantee to work. I have to say that because I don't know who is really going to do it the right way where it could possibly work but I do know a great deal of people who have applied this tactic to their life and had scary amazing results from doing so. Some saw results fast and many didn't see anything manifest until years and years later, but they never swayed away from the principle and continued to apply it. What I am talking about is the usage of vision boards or visuals.

For years many successful people have credited using a visual of some sort to manifest the success they have obtained. Some use post-it's on their bathroom mirror with words that they say to themselves at the start of each day. Some place a picture of the house they would like to live in someday on their computer or the car they would like to drive on the fridge so every time they go to grab something to eat or drink, they are reminded what they want to see in the driveway. I have even heard stories of those who would drive pass the house that they wanted to buy every day and would imagine themselves turning the key to go inside until the day came that they were the owners of that home. I have personally used vision boards as well that spoke of the income I wanted to make monthly to the areas I wanted to live in or even the idea of driving a newer car. I've even gone as far as visualizing my steering wheel holding the emblem of a car that I wanted. Like I stated earlier, it works for some and for others not so much. The primary reason I believe that it doesn't work for some is simply a lack of belief in what you see.

It goes back to the statement I made at the beginning of the chapter when I asked how many blessings have we talked ourselves out of over the years. I'm sure that I am not alone when I say I've heard this statement time and time again from many individuals…"I have to see it to believe it." That single statement alone has murdered trillions on top of trillions of dreams since the beginning of time! You are basically saying out loud that since I can't see it then that means it's not real. And guess what? You will get exactly what you asked for. The bible says that God made us in His likeness. What does that mean? In the beginning everything was created by God simply speaking it. There was no explosion of molecules and a loud noise from atoms colliding and then there everything was. He spoke it. He stood on nothing and created everything. Then we were created and given the same power and authority to speak and claim the very things that we want and depending on your level of faith backing your verbal provision will determine how fast you see the results. A lot of times we are waiting for "that thing" we asked for to just fall into our lap and it doesn't always work exactly like that. It could simply be a situation where you attend a party or event and meet someone who lines you up with the very person you need to talk to for "that thing" to manifest itself. At times, it could mean that someone you know has what you want and by you simply speaking it out loud and believing that you will have it, places your name on their heart and they give you a "random" call and during the conversation realize that you are the very one they are supposed to sell that house to or fill that position with. If nothing else, can you at least practice this principle for the next couple of years and truly apply your thoughts and heart into what you say and be very careful and cautious about what you speak in reference to your goals or dreams. If nothing has worked so far then why not give it a try? The worst that could happen has already been happening if everything you've wanted has avoided you so now let's try something different and seek to change the narrative.

So this thought just hit me like a ton of bricks. What if the very thing you been wanting is sitting right under you and the only reason that you can't see it is because you haven't mentioned that you even want it? Let me explain with a story about a really good friend of mine. My guy is a very spiritual man who practiced these very principles to become successful in real estate. I'm talking about he has spoken out loud how much money he wanted to make a month which is more than what he used to make a year on his last job before he became an entrepreneur. He had these huge dreams that he would manifest by speaking over and over again and after some time he would meet the right people that knew the right people and then

BOOM!! The very thing he kept speaking on would come to fruition. Another story is one from my personal experience that goes back to 2014. During that time, I was working in pest control and I had a busted up Pontiac that I drove that made this loud noise when I would drive that would draw attention every time that I came pass someone. After a while, I grew tired of feeling embarrassed about it so I mentally tricked myself into seeing the emblem on my steering wheel as either a sports car that I liked or even an exotic car that I could only dream of driving. So now when I drove pass someone and they would look around like as if to say, 'what is that', in my mind they were looking at my 'nice' car and impressed with what they saw. Funny, I know but it was definitely a confidence booster for sure and at the time I could have won an Oscar for how much I convinced myself that I was no longer in that Pontiac when clearly that wasn't the case. One day, I took it a step further. With my little income and poor credit, I decided to start speaking out loud that at the turn of the new year I would go to a car lot and leave with a new car. I had absolutely no clue how that was going to happen as the next year was only six months away. But it didn't stop me from visualizing my car was something else other than what it was and speaking what I planned to do at the beginning of 2015. So, things began to happen. I met a guy that offered certain services such as credit repair, which I had never done before, and I became heavily involved in network marketing. One thing led to the next (all the while I'm still claiming my goal for a new car at the beginning of 2015) and before the end of the year I was looking at a credit score of 722 and had a small residual income coming from the network marketing business which, when added to my full time income, I was sitting pretty. But, going into 2015, none of this played in my head as a product of manifestation. Keep in mind, I had never stopped claiming what I wanted. I got a call from a friend who was in the same network marketing business that needed some help with moving his business further. He asked me to meet him at his job as he would have a bunch of down time one day in particular. He just so happened to work at a car dealership. Not thinking anything of it, I go and meet with him on the day that he asked which was January 5th, 2015. We talked for a minute and then he looks at my busted up Pontiac and says, "Man when are you going to get out that thing?" We laughed about it and he suggests I check to see what my credit score was and maybe he could help me out.

Up until this time, it had not even registered that everything I spoke was transpiring. He comes back and says, "with your income and credit you can leave today with a brand new car and not pay a single cent down if you wish". Long story short, I drove away an owner of two new cars, zero down! Talking about overzealous, huh? It wasn't until I left the lot that it dawned on me what just happened. I manifested the very thing I said I would do.

Maybe there is fund lingering with your name on it that you need to verbally claim to get access to or maybe your credit is better than it needs to be to get the very house you want but because you haven't said anything, you haven't received the right call yet. There may be a dream spouse for you somewhere or a dream job that you feel underqualified for at the time. Maybe you want to get your kids in a private school, but not sure how to get the funds for it. There are many things that people want and wish for every day but settle for the idea that they are just mere thoughts and nothing will ever transpire from them. I disagree. They are not just thoughts, but they are your desires and you can have what you wish or get close enough to something in that arena simply from speaking it in existence. The biggest key is believing what your mouth and mind says and not your eyes. Trust that your words can bring anything you speak to life and watch what happens. Your words have power. Time to use it.

CHAPTER 3

LOOK UP

This chapter is probably the most important in the entire book. I want to discuss two very key reasons why you can be successful. What's crazy is you would probably think that I'm going to say something extremely profound and deep! And before I say it, I will even go a step further and say that these two principles are the **LAST** things most people seem to think about as it relates to them gaining more knowledge and streamlining to their success.

When I was a kid, I used to live next door to my great aunt. I called her Aunt Lucy and she was my grandfather's aunt. Every time I went outside to play, she was either sitting in her rocking chair knitting something on the porch, doing yard work, or talking to a neighbor. But she was always active and never seemed to sit still for a lady her age. I would occasionally go over and do a task for her and then she would talk to me for hours about different things. One of the most important talks we had was when she taught me to always find someone who knows more than I did and learn as much as I could from them. "Only a fool would not ask someone for help", is something she might have said to me. She was a woman of a great deal of wisdom. She was an aunt to a couple well known politicians and many of the people I saw come visit her were prominent in the things they did.

So she was always in communication with very intelligent and driven people. I never forgot that principle. Always look for those that know more than myself and learn as much as I can.

So the first principle I want to discuss is the importance of shadowing and finding a mentor. At every job or business that I have ever been involved with, I became known as the guy that was extra. What do I mean by that you ask? Well, let's use my last job for example. I worked with a pest control company for over six years in the sales department handling deals with customers all over the United States. When I started the job, everyone goes through a four to five week training class where we are taught different things the job will require us to know in order to be successful. Well, when dealing with pest control one of the most vital things one must learn is the nature and pattern of insects. Where they live, what they like, what they hate, why they do this and why they do that. We have to be very knowledgeable about their mating habits, the process with how they lay eggs, and even the times of the year and locations of your home they may be more prone to be attracted to so that we can determine over the phone simply from a customer's verbal illustration what the pest issue could possibly be. To say that training wasn't thorough would be a flat out lie. I had some amazing trainers during the time that I attended training. Then came the time for Q & A. The time where you as a trainee should express the areas of concern you have so that these issues could be addressed before you reached the sales floor and go live. What was the question I had? Who are the top two salespeople on the floor is what I wanted to know. I retract. I NEEDED to know. See in my mind, I was going to go out there and study their habits for a bit and then when the time was right, I would inquire about one or two things at a time and piece together how they did things in order to be successful. The way I figured, if I take the best methods from one and the best from the other and put them together, I've just created a super salesman and it would be practically impossible to not be successful. Another thing I did (which is the reason I said I was extra) is watch tons of videos on insects. I wanted to know what it looked like, no matter how disgusting, it was when they did anything so as a customer explained what they saw over the phone, these were the images I had in my mind to match the description. I even went as far as talking to pest technicians that I knew to get more insight on the pesky little creatures. How did it pan out? I worked in three different sales departments during my time there. In all six years I only saw the top five in rankings for each department, I was awarded a trip to the Dominican Republic for top salespeople and won tons of prizes for sales accomplishments which included appliances, gift cards, and extra bonuses that at times were as big as the weekly check or bigger. I consistently stayed in the top percentage of salespeople each month in six years which is almost impossible in competitive sales environments especially when you are competing with TONS of people in your office and sometimes, depending on your team, had to include the agents at the other sites as well. I was never afraid to "look up" the top people in each department and pick their brains and "look up" additional information that wasn't included in the original training to maximize the results of my position. So that's the first key to becoming successful. Follow the ones that are already winning and learn their "secret".

The next thing that you should do, which could be controversial depending on your beliefs which I highly encourage you to skim to the next chapter if you choose, is "look up" to God. So why is this step the second key to becoming successful and not the first? Very simple. Because when you pray, one of the most direct ways to pray for anything is to be so intentional that you call things out by name. So, going back to the first key which I stated was finding out who knows more than you and picking their brain, I recommend that once you get the name of these persons to pray that 'Charlie' or whatever their name may be, has the heart to share with you the things that have helped him and even cover his well-being? Being intentional with your prayers instead of vague provides God with the exact thing (even though He already knows) your heart desires. You leave nothing to chance but call out the very thing you want. If you desire a house in five years, state the month and year you want it, the location (address if you have it), type of yard you would like, the neighbors you want, and even the color of the house you prefer. Even though there are no guarantees that you will get that particular house, once you speak everything in the atmosphere that you really would like, you'll be surprised how much more often than not most of the boxes get checked. But the biggest of all within this key is believing the very prayer that you just made.

It doesn't matter what you have prayed for. The bottom line is you have to see it in your mind even while praying for it. Looking up to God requires more than your voice but also your heart. A lot of us need to do a 'heart check' on ourselves to make sure we truly believe that the things we desire are possible. As a man thinketh so is he. That has never been more truer. I have noticed that every time someone tells me what they can't learn or do, I quickly notice that they aren't lying. They never learn whatever it is. If someone ever tells me what they KNOW they can't have for whatever reason, I have yet to see them later in time and hear that they actually got the very thing they claimed they would never have. I'm not saying it can't happen…just that I haven't seen it.

These two steps have made all the difference in my life. When talking with people whom you find successful in the arena you have interest in learning about, you will be amazed how much most of these individuals really enjoy sharing the wealth. I can't really recall anytime I asked someone a question about how they obtained success, wealth, or simply for their strategy and was not awarded with the answer I was looking for. In either situation, whether talking with someone or talking with God, the same principle stands...a closed mouth don't get fed! You have to be willing to speak up for what you want. Being successful is not a one time thing. It is a continuous process that requires constant learning, developing, adapting, and maneuvering, so you may as well get used to being uncomfortable early on since your new norm will be to find comfort in the uncomfortable. Those that do this faster usually find the finish line the fastest. Be that guy. Be that gal. Be the one that people look at and say they are so extra because they want to go above and beyond what's been given. Be the one that eventually is the name being called as the top of their field and watch how many come to pick your brain the same way you did to get where you're going. Be focused. Be direct. Be intentional. And look up!

CHAPTER 4

MAKE A DECISION

When you really sit back and think about your life and look at all the things you have and even the things you don't, it comes down to one common denominator…everything we have or not is a result of a decision that we made. Where we live. The car we drive. The spouse that we married. The career or job that we currently utilize for income. All of these things are a product of a decision or a series of decisions. I mean, think about it. What if you met your spouse in college? This is the same person you have been with for the last fifteen years. Since you guys have been together, you have chosen a home and cars and maybe had children. Looking at this scenario I want you to step back and think of this logic…what if you made the decision to go to a different college? Changes the entire dynamics of the last fifteen years huh? But wait, there's another logic. Assuming that you love the life you have currently with this person as your spouse, what do you think those same fifteen years would have looked like without them if you simply said, "I don't really know what I want to do with my life", and instead of just jumping out the nest and learning to fly on the way down by going to college, which is where you met them, you "decided" (or lack thereof) to stay home for two to four years and work dead end jobs to get by just to stay busy? Do you see what just happened here? The life you currently love would be non-existent had you not simply 'made a decision' early on.

So you're probably asking what does this have to do with anything goal related or business related? The answer is it has to do with everything. When we make it a habit to just float through life haphazardly and live by the motto, "whatever happens…happens", then we are subject to live the life that we would least admire. The thing is 'something' has to happen. Either you make a decision that leads to the happening or the bare minimum available is what you are left with. In the end, do you really want the bare minimum options available for a spouse or lover based solely on the environment that you are in that is consistent with your lack of decision making or would you like your place and position in life to constantly put you in the best situations because you continue to chose 'ideal' circumstances for yourself which means your environment will also be conducive to such.

When we don't make a decision on whether or not to fix our credit, we are leaving it up to chance where we get to live. A simple decision to work on your credit score means you have the option to get an apartment or buy a house versus only being subject to an apartment or rental home because you haven't placed yourself in the right position for home ownership. When we make a decision on which career path or business we would like to partake in, we set ourselves up to study information pertaining to the path in which we chose in order to become better in our skillset. Otherwise, we keep ending up with jobs that we hate because we have let uncertainty decide for us what is available to maintain survival, which we have already discussed it will be the bare minimum options accessible usually.

At the end of the day, either you live by chance or you make a decision. The scary truth is most decisions, though some may be more simple than others, usually take us down a path that cannot be altered or changed for years to come so it's very important to consider all options and the consequences that may follow whether good or bad and if you are willing to live with the results.

I wholeheartedly believe that 75% of the world are not living the life that they truly desire. That number may be higher or lower as this is from no research but merely a product of my own judgment, but I truly think that many of us have picked what was easily and readily available for us from fear of working towards the unknown or simply not wanting to deal with the energy of putting forth a great deal of effort to create the life we want.

When I see doctors, lawyers, pilots, engineers, military personnel, entrepreneurs, or teachers just to name a few because there are way more careers we could point out, I tend to have a deeper appreciation for what they do not because of their actual job task or description of duty, but merely because these are typically careers that an individual has to sit and map out in their mind that this is what I am going to do. These aren't the businesses or careers that a person usually just fall into without some type of "wanting" to involve themselves in these areas. A decision was definitely made. Even if it was a situation that led them to only having these options available, it doesn't take much energy to say no and try to 'figure it out' another way which usually doesn't end up placing you in ideal positions in the long haul. But these careers right here and some others are typically the very ones led by individuals who want to be there. Think about the level of stress that may come with some of these. No one deals with that type of stress unless it's voluntary meaning they desire to make an impact some way, some how in these careers. These usually are not for the faint of heart, but then again deciding on anything important in life isn't going to be done by someone that's faint of heart. Which is why it's time that you 'make a decision' to take control of your life so that you can truly have different results.

One of the most over-used statements that I absolutely despise is when someone says that they are a product of their environment. Woooooo how that makes my water boil hearing that crap! Listen, every single person born has an environment that surrounds them. Some better than others of course, but yet and still we are all to some degree products of an environment. Just because someone is born into a family with a 7,000 square foot house doesn't mean they didn't deal with some type of abuse, alcoholism, drugs, or negative energy of some sort while growing up. So, you see someone was raised in a two-parent home where both parents worked two jobs and never did drugs and only showed love, you would probably say there is no way that environment could be bad, but at the same time what if the parents were never available for the child's school activities or sporting events or a simple day date to the movies or the carnival? Do you think this child grows up appreciating that "environment" where they felt neglected, unimportant, and unwanted? I would like to say no as none of us want to deal with that type of situation as a child which sadly many of us have that same story in our own repertoire that we could share as well. The point I'm making in all of this is that your environment has nothing to do with the decision you make for yourself. Simply allowing your surroundings to 'justify' your actions is a flat-out excuse. Nothing more.

I have several guys that I grew up with that are doing phenomenal in life as we speak and their "environment" does not spell anything that these men are currently doing in the world. I have one brother that grew up in a neighborhood called Hyde Park where for years have been riddled with crime, drugs, and hopelessness. Most of the city of Memphis would vouch that they dare not stop anywhere for anything in that neighborhood unless they absolutely had too for some reason outside of their control. Yet this brother of mine, who was surrounded by drugs and violence his entire life in this neighborhood, does not possess a criminal record as he has never touched drugs a day in his life, does not smoke nor consume any drugs of any kind, and every year life clockwork puts on a charity event in that very neighborhood where he hosts Christian music artists, bounce houses for the children, free food, activities, and gives away hundreds of backpacks with supplies inside of them to the children of that area. Now knowing what I said about his 'environment' to be true, would this be the type of energy you would think this area would produce? Absolutely not! Then what makes his actions so different from the actions of those he was surrounded by growing up...his decision. That's it. Plain and simple. He made a decision to do something about it. One that would be different for the kids coming up to see so that they can make a choice of their own. Now they can say we will sell and do drugs OR we want to help bless others just like us since we know that's an option. See, sometimes your decision can change the landscape of an 'environment'. The very thing that you chose to do differently could create a ripple effect through those around you and now, ten years later, we could be making an entirely different storyline about the place that you call home.

What are you going to do about it? About your life, your passions, your desires, your environment, and the very things you believe you aspire to accomplish. Will they be left up to chance or are you ready to throw rocks in the water to create movement? Nothing happens until you happen and if you decide not to move, then the very things you do not want is what takes precedence. Let's change the status quo of your life with the utilization of one word...decision. Don't worry about the results that we cannot see right now. Just the simple thought of what's possible should be your only focus. Work hard and intentionally on creating what you want to see and the only results that could occur would still be in that avenue. You have power over your thoughts and control over your actions. Put those two together and make a choice to be what you desire and not a byproduct of what's available at the bottom of the barrel. You were created to be great. Think about it. Your life can be what YOU say regardless of where you are from. You don't see the power in that? Surely, you do. That's why after reading this book you are going to make a decision and watch some things begin to change.

CHAPTER 5

KILL THE OUTSIDE NOISE

For many of us, we have found the hardest thing in life to overcome is chastisement. Sometimes it's for our own good that we receive it based on the reasoning behind where it comes from, but then there are times when it simply comes from the person closest to us not understanding what it is we are doing or trying to accomplish in life. I've come to notice that many dreams and goals for individuals have been put on hold or called off due to a degree of verbal discouragement received from some of their closest friends, family, or lovers. Many times they seek validation more than the results of the hard work and effort they put in to achieve positive results in their mission or assignment. I spoke on this in an earlier chapter that we have got to find a way to see past validation of others and seek only the great results from hitting our goals.

Remembering the "why" you are doing something is far greater than any validation that could take place. There is a strong force in your life that whether you speak on it or not gets you out of bed in the morning. This same energy is what drives you to work overtime, miss meals, skip out of activities with family and friends, and drive you constantly seeking resolve in achieving what your heart has set out to see happen. Your "why" should be the only validation you need to keep going. People are going to talk about you whether you are doing great or poorly. You have got to understand today that everyone standing in your corner is not there by their own placement. We have grabbed hands and walked individuals to our corners against their own will hoping and wishing that these people would want our best interests attained. Not everyone with you is for you and not everything spoken about you is true. This is something that you are going to have to place in your mind as a solid fact and not fiction. There has to be a level of understanding within yourself to know that every handclap is not in your favor more so than it is those individuals don't want to be caught sitting still while others around you are giving a standing ovation. You have to know that every hand shake and pat on the back does not happen willingly without a knife in the unseen hand. You have to believe that in the end you will see who is truly for you and those that are against you, but needless to say, none of that should matter at this moment. Why? Because you have work to do.

Until you get to a place where your vision is starting to manifest itself, you have to ignore the negative and positive feedback. The reason is because you don't want to focus so much on what anyone is saying, good or bad, because it could cloud your steps. The human mind works best when focused solely on one thing at a time. That does not mean a person can't be successful at multitasking. That is not what I am saying. What I am saying is you must develop laser focus on the task at hand in order to achieve maximum results and not have too much side work going on that could take time, energy, and mental power from what you are really looking to accomplish.

That is why I say block out the outside noise. Not all noise in your direction is bad. Some could be cheering but until you cross the finish line you can't let up off the gas to wave at the cheerleaders. Until you see the refs throw their hands up to signal touchdown, you can't get halfway there to do your dance because you hear cheering. Throughout the noise you still have work to do. You still have an assignment that must be finished. You still have results that you demand to witness.

I believe that in order to be successful in whatever it is that you are doing there are four requirements that you must have in your arsenal to get pass the finish line. I will not only tell you what these key pieces are, but I'll also break down why they are so important to have.

The first of the four is tunnel vision. What exactly is tunnel vision? Some of the definitions that I've looked up describing tunnel vision say that is it peripheral vison loss, or in other words, the lack of ability to see what are to the sides with the only visibility being what's directly ahead. Another definition described it as a vision "defect" where objects cannot be seen UNLESS they are front and center of your focus or visual field. In either definition the fact remains the same…what's not your center focus should not and cannot be seen. You have to get to a place where nothing beside or behind you can move you. In your mind, those directions don't even exist. The only thing you see is the end zone. For those that don't follow football, this is the area where the player has to get to in order to score a touchdown. Because of the design of football helmets, you have to literally turn your head away from the end zone to see who is beside and behind you. There are a number of blind spots for a football player to deal with on their way to score a touchdown. The greatest players are the ones who develop a "feel" for what is going on around them and knowing where to go to avoid failure to score that touchdown. This is what you must have in order to win big in life. You need to develop the ability to know that there are things to the left of you that want to see you fall and there are things to the right of you that need to hold you up a bit in effort to slow you down, but in both scenarios, you should know how to keep going and dodging these situations while maintaining focus on the end zone.

The second key to have is thick skin. Why is this so important? When it comes to blocking out the outside noise, one of the most dynamic reasons that cause many people to fall off is not knowing how to handle the things said about them. There will be a time when someone who you believe is your greatest supporter will, for whatever reason, say something about you that may be toxic enough to destroy your feelings. I have heard some of the worse things a person could think being said about me behind my back from a small few of the very people I love dearly. They didn't understand my vision and the direction I was going because, as most would know, especially if you have started a new journey to do something that you believe is great, you will encounter a ton of setbacks. Many of these setbacks will and can be devastating to say the least. What makes an individual great is their ability to drive straight through the devastation and find a way out to the light. To those on the outside looking in, it makes absolutely no sense to go through any of that when there is an easier way to live. This is why the status quo is overpopulated. Because so many don't fight for their goals and dreams from fear of running into what's hard and not easy. The very moment that you make a decision to go through the wall to get to what's on the other side, the average persons that do not understand, whether they are friend or family member, will have their say on why you shouldn't do what's hard when you can "survive" just fine on what's easy. It's just sometimes the way they express this concern comes off a little harsh. What we have to do as conquerors is see their "concern" as what it is and simply entitle it as lack of understanding and continue to move forward. Do not allow the distraction of words place center blocks in your path. Step over them, dust off your shoes, and keep it moving.

The third thing a successful person must have is an unlimited second wind. Second wind is more commonly known to occur in sports or physical training. Second wind is defined as a phenomenon in running or sports where the athlete (person) who is out of breath and too tired to continue suddenly finds the strength to press on at top performance with less exertion. Before you continue reading, go back and reread that definition. The definition alone should be enough explanation as to why this key is so imperative to have in order to achieve massive success. The idea that one can be so exhausted that they cannot continue, but suddenly as the definition described, they can find wind/strength/energy out of absolutely nowhere to finish (not casually) but at top performance is truly an amazing gift to have. There will come times during your journey that will test your mental endurance. Things will happen outside of your control. Situations will occur that you cannot fix or would take an extreme battle to overcome. Then there will be those moments that you would feel you have gone over a million miles to have achieved only fifteen steps. This is where second wind kicks in. When you are ready to tap out and submit you have to find that extra "deep breath" and go back in and finish. It won't be cute. It won't feel pleasant. It won't be gentle. But then again this is not what you are fighting for. You aren't looking for cute, pleasant, and gentle results. You are looking to win. Period. And in the process of winning, you have to invite and welcome all the uncomfortable feelings so that you have something to step on to get closer to the top.

The last key that you must possess in order to be successful is passion. When you think of the word passion as it relates to goals and dreams, you should envision a feeling of euphoria when it comes to thinking about the end result of your journey. This thing that you want so desperately to accomplish is only this drastic to you because of your passion. Countries have been conquered because of one man's passion. Championships have been won by the less talented team because of passion. Businesses have opened and thrived because of the owner's passion. If you haven't caught on by now then let me spill the beans and let you in on a secret. Passion brings victory. It does not matter how hard the road may be or how long the task may take. It isn't based upon the talent level you have to achieve whatever the goal is. It has always been known since the beginning of time that if there is anything someone is passionate about, chances are they will achieve it. Period. Passion can move a mountain. The very way we were created was from "passion". Think about that. Life itself is a result of passion. No matter how you slice it, you must find passion in what you are doing or it will not succeed. There has to be a feeling of accomplishment long before the accomplishment actually takes place. Just the thought of doing what you love without even being close to the finish line should give you the same feeling as if you'd already completed the tasks at hand. Embrace the process. Love every aspect of what you have to go through and deal with in effort to achieve the results you envisioned. This is your journey to enjoy. No one has to like it except you. Do what you need to do to win, but make sure you do it with tunnel vision, thick skin, unlimited second wind, and most importantly passion.

CHAPTER 6

BE INTENTIONAL

There was a time some years ago when I was just like the majority of people and did things hoping and wishing for a good outcome, but not really believing it until I saw it. I still hear people say that phrase today that has remained a popular coined excuse for years now. You may have heard it before or used it yourself from time to time, but boy were we wrong. It goes a little something like this, "I'll believe it when I see it." I really wish I could actually see the blessings and good endings that were lost because of these words. Like if I could really tap into the spiritual realm to see where I may have missed out on a car when I didn't qualify for it, but intentional belief would have obtained it for me or the times when I may have come up on a financial blessing but missed out because I didn't believe anything good was coming my way at the moment. I wish I knew what I really missed from simply operating in pure, uncut nonbelief. The way I see it, if things don't look promising at the moment, what do I really have to lose anyway? Just intentionally speak what you want, believe it by seeing yourself with it mentally, and patiently wait for it to manifest itself if it be so. It's not like it takes away from anything by imagining that you have already obtained whatever it is that you want. The worst case scenario is that things stay the same and nothing happens and the best case scenario is that the very thing you spoke and thought heavily about actually becomes your reality. Whichever the case, be intentional with your words and thoughts. But especially your words.

Another important way that one can be intentional is through action. I am beyond guilty of what I'm about to tell you. How many times have you had a major project that you'd given yourself or let's just say a very important goal and you had a deadline in which you wanted to accomplish the task? In each of those situations, how many times did you designate time for that project and found yourself doing everything else the entire time and only spent maybe 40-50% of that allotted time on your assignment at hand? What happened? How did something so important that we had to assign a certain time to get it done get so entangled with everything else we had going on in life at the moment to the point where what was important took a backseat to things that were obsolete? It's simple. We were not being intentional with the task at hand. The definition of intentional is for something to be done on purpose and deliberate. Another definition I saw stated that when you are intentional, you CHOOSE to make decisions and take action on what's important to you by being clear and upfront about what you want to achieve. Translation-nothing else matters except that one thing!

We have got to get in a position where we kill the outside noise, make a decision on what needs to be done, and intentionally get it done! That simple. Nothing should have precedence over what's important especially if your future is on the line. I look at it this way. If we always have one eye somewhere else in the event that what we want to happen doesn't pan out, how much more likely will it be true that the very thing we want will fail? I ask this because it's hard to give 100% of your attention when 20% of your vision is somewhere else. You want "A" results with "C" effort and focus. You can never give your all if only half of you is available. Be intentional. See nothing else except that one thing. Show no attention to outside distractions. Turn your phone off, go somewhere quiet if you can, and if you can't put your earphones in and drown out the chaos around you, but whatever you do just remember to stay focused and keep pressing forward.

The final way you can be intentional that I want to discuss is very vital. Even so, the bible stresses this as a means of showing that you are coming into wisdom. When I have an important task or goal that I want to complete, I make it a point to write things out almost like a map, giving direction as to when I would do this and do that so that my steps are guided. Not only do I write it out and create a plan, but I have accountability partners that know what I'm reaching for and their only assignment is to segue me back to the task if I sway. They are a very important piece to success because as you may know life can and will definitely happen and the smallest distraction can throw you off for weeks and sometimes months at a time. But if you have key accountability partners that see to it that you remain focused on the goal and stay active with the plan, it becomes easier to regroup and jump back on the horse than if you were at this thing alone. The bible says a wise man is he who listens to counsel and accepts discipline. Your accountability partners will challenge you at times when you least feel like hearing it and it will be times where they will not be your most favorite people. But you are not in this for your feelings and their job isn't to monitor yours. You have them in place to see you at your weakest point and direct you back to where you need to be in order to finish the assignment. Find someone that you can trust to be blunt, open, and dependable. This is someone who knows the strings to pull and buttons to push to get your reaction, but in a positive way. They are your personal motivators that will not let up no matter how much you cry about it. They are only done when the job is done. Be intentional with who you give this authority to because this could be one of the most important pieces to your approach to being intentional.

Life can seem extremely difficult at times for so many individuals. Then you have the select few that seem to skate through unscathed. I'm willing to bet that most of the ones that seem to get by untouched and unbothered are the main ones who speak and believe what they want without seeing it in front of them. They are the most intentional people I know. They will tell you that they are going to do something and even place a timeline on it and have no clue how it's going to get done yet in their minds, there is nothing stopping them from achieving the goal. There is a lot to learn from these people of faith. Thing is, we all possess this gift. We all have the ability to see and say what we truly desire and walk this thing out until it happens. Stop worrying about what your friends say about it. Be intentional. Stop focusing on the barriers that keep slowing down your progress. Be intentional. Stop caring about how long the journey has taken you. Be intentional. Quit looking at the fact you barely have half of the resources needed to get the job done. Be intentional. Learn very fast how to develop tunnel vision and selective hearing so that nothing can stop or sway you from what you believe is yours to obtain. Simply be intentional and keep swinging. Eventually you'll hit the homerun.

CHAPTER 7

BE GRATEFUL

When I sit back and really think about what it means to be grateful, something that keeps coming to mind is humility. Even though the two are somewhat different, they are still very closely connected. In both situations, whether grateful or humble, I've noticed the same outcome…increase!

There are studies that have been performed by some well-known psychological research teams that have associated gratitude with increases in happiness, health, financial growth, the ability to maintain peace longer, and better relationships with people and businesses. When a person is truly grateful, they appreciate the situation they are in regardless of the outcome and rarely would you hear them complain or speak grudgingly against things they have to do even when they don't want to. In a nutshell, they respect the process. An individual displaying high gratitude in a situation isn't saying that they are choosing to settle in the moment, but what they are saying (through their attitude) that they are just passing through and their current position will not have power over their mood, decision-making abilities, or their peace. They understand that it takes steps to get where they want to go and sometimes those steps lead them into no man's land, an area that nobody feels comfortable in and probably some of the lowest points in the process to becoming better or successful.

I truly appreciate the fact that I have been surrounded by some pretty grateful people in my life that have taught me to always find the beauty within the ugly. I knew someone who was confined to a bed, as he couldn't walk nor feed himself, and he would joke about the fact that he always wanted to be fed like a king. He totally disregarded the fact of why he was having to be fed, but instead saw the joy of knowing every meal would be fed to him. You have people that show happiness while performing certain tasks at work that most people would despise and their reasoning for being happy is the fact that they have a job that helps them provide and they aren't unemployed. Some people have experienced some painful circumstances in life, but they would tell you that they would rather be alive and figure out how to deal with it than be dead and not have life's problems at all.

Not only having gratitude is important, but as I said before, humility plays a major role in increase in a person's life. It is with humility, many times, that a person shows the most self-respect for themselves and those around them. A quote by Saint Augustine goes, "It was pride that changed angels into devils; it is humility that makes men as angels". When people see your humility, they want to support you even more. They recognize a person of valor and integrity that can be trusted and usually what happens is, especially in business, those individuals don't get the promotion based on skillset more than they do from simple attitude and how they carry themselves. I know I made the joke earlier about my old Pontiac being busted and disgusted and how I would envision that it was another car, but don't get it twisted and think I didn't appreciate that car. It got me where I needed to go and I didn't have to catch a bus anymore like I did prior to getting the car. I would rather hear the loud noises of my own car than to continue hearing the noises and smelling the odors that I did while riding the public bus. In every situation there is a good that can be pulled out and appreciated. There is always something that can serve as a reminder that it could be worse. In the process of showing gratitude for those things one would usually notice how things start falling into place little by little. Sometimes it could be a fast change in your life and others experience years of waiting for their breakthrough, but usually when it comes, it brings a joy that more than supersedes the time they spent in their "moment of gratitude" while they waited.

Being grateful helps you in many ways that go undocumented. Your blood pressure stays lower because you aren't stressed. Your thoughts are sharper and your decision are clearer because you aren't distracted by the circumstances. You are friendlier to others which leads them to want to be around you and help you more. You have a stronger level of patience that helps you wait out the time needed to get to the next level. If you don't do anything else, practice being grateful more. Take notes of the things you complain about more than others and write beside it the one good thing that is in each of those situations. Don't have too much pride to find the good. Some would be like, "oh there is nothing good about this or that", but truth be told there is at least 1% of good in everything bad or uncomfortable. When you find it, write it down, and focus on that one thing while you wait for better to appear. Remember, we can't control a lot of outcomes in life, but the one thing we can control no matter what the issue is how we perceive it and respond. Your response is your responsibility and no one or nothing can make you feel any way you don't agree to feel. See it for what it is, recognize what you really want, and focus on the idea that it could be worse as a reminder that you aren't completely at the bottom. I guarantee that gratitude and humility will be the game changers in your life.

CHAPTER 8

PRAY

When people say, "pray about it", what do you think they really mean? What does the process consist of and how long does it go on? When is the best time to do? Does it work for everything or only some things? How does prayer work when it comes to being successful? Is it something that helps everyone and if so, why doesn't everyone just pray for success so that they can get it? Should others pray with me or should do it alone? What words do I say and how do I know if God is listening? I know you're probably wondering why I said all this but believe it or not these are some of the questions I have encountered from others in reference to prayer and praying for what they desire. I have this phrase I like to use called 'intentional praying' where I call out exactly what I want and preference a time frame as to when I would like it. I try not to be as vague as many of the prayers you may have heard in the past where one may simply asked to be blessed and not really specify what it actually means to them when they say, 'be blessed'. As far as God is concerned you were blessed to be alive and say the prayer so what other blessing could you speak of outside of that. It's not that He doesn't know your heart, but at the same time your prayer should be direct and intentional so that action could take place specifically for what you are praying for.

Think about why you should be intentional with your prayers. If someone is sick and you pray for them, would you want their blessing to be dinner for the next night or healing? If someone is looking for a job promotion and they ask you to send one up to God for them, should you ask that they get approved for a car? Sounds really crazy right? Well think about the spirit world for a second. If your words hold power and your words are vague with no real topic or direction, how are your prayers supposed to be applied if you don't specifically make it plain and clear what you are speaking of? Let's normalize being direct with our words when we pray. So many blessings are tied up because Holy Spirit don't know when to release them to you. Most importantly, it's not always the idea that you will get what you are asking for more than the idea that your steps will be ordered so that you might end up at the right place at the right time with the right knowledge and skillset obtained to handle the very blessing that you are praying for. Many times, we simply just need to know what to do and our actions will handle the rest. But God is waiting for you to include Him so that He can lead you in the right direction and stop you from being so frivolous in your actions while working to secure your dreams.

Moment of clarity. I realize that some don't have the same beliefs or belief system that I may have. I get that. But what I do know is that regardless what anyone may or may not believe, we all answer to something. How many times has the car not started and whether you believed in God or not, you screamed, "COME ON! DON'T DO THIS TO ME! CRANK UP BABY! COME ON NOW!"

Who were you talking too? The car isn't alive, is it? What about when you are about to do something important and you try to hype yourself up by saying, "You got this Rod. You can do this. The test will be nothing to you. This interview will be a breeze. Easy does it and it's all yours boy. Let's get it done!" Well if you are you and you are telling you what you can do then are you implying that you have the power to make it happen whatever the something is? Don't get lost in the continuous use of the word 'you' but see what I'm suggesting here. You speak directly to the car saying exactly what you don't want it to do, but what you desire for it to do instead. You specifically gave the car a command. The key word is 'specifically'. While hyping yourself up, you give authority to yourself through your words by saying what's possible and suggesting the effortlessness that it will take to get it done. Whether this is fact or not, you were intentional with your words.

Now I will take it a step further and say this. Even if you don't believe, what will it hurt to simply try it. You will do it alone in the comfort of your personal space and you can speak as freely as you wish because no one will hear you. You speak with intention on things anyway, so just add this to the equation. Worst case scenario, things stay the same and nothing happens as it probably would have been anyway or maybe, just maybe, something shifts. I can boldly say the last two sentences with confidence because I have witnessed shifts happening as a result of prayer. Jobs I should not have had and cars I should have not been approved for where a result of intentional prayer. I have spoken of having a certain knowledge for something in particular and as time went by I would 'suddenly' meet people in different walks of life that had the knowledge of a subject matter that I was asking for in my prayer time. I have had sicknesses that I took no medicine for, but simply spoke the illness out of my body and after a couple days I was well. I have spoken of procedures that I wanted a company to perform in my favor that went against what they would normally do in those situations, and one time in particular I was with my brother Polo and he heard my prayer as he was getting in the car. Right after I prayed, I called the company on speaker phone and he heard the lady say, "Mr.Shipp, I don't know why I'm doing this because this is not what we do in this situation, but we will handle it as you suggested and we look forward to speaking with you again in a week from today." He could only look at me in pure disbelief as to what he just witnessed. He watched me call in existence what I wanted to happen. Does this happen all the time. Absolutely NOT! Not even 50% of the time. But if just below half the time you speak on something and it happens as you said, would you not take the chance as often as humanly possible to speak all things that you desire through prayer?

See the key ingredient that continuous prayer produces is called faith. The more you pray and believe what you are praying for, the stronger your faith becomes. It is with your faith that things take precedence with your words because faith is the language of God. Well, Rod, if I don't believe in God how can I ever have faith? You believe in God and don't even know it. I say this because you operate by His principles every single day whether you believe it or not. How? Well, let me ask you this. How many times have you just sat down in a chair and hesitated because you were afraid the legs would not hold your weight? You don't, do you? You just sit down without thinking twice about the strength and durability of the chair. When you get in the car, you don't think twice that the inside of the car could just bottom out while you are driving 85 mph on the interstate. Why? Because you have FAITH! You have faith in a chair and in the frame of the car. You have faith that the food you eat will not make you sick. You have faith that both traffic lights won't turn green at the same time. You have faith that your heating system will not spill out carbon monoxide but perform as it's designed. You have faith that the ground won't open up as you walk and swallow you inside. There's nothing stopping the ground from giving in while you walk, but your faith suggests that you will be just fine. Your faith tells you that when you close your eyes at night that you will wake up in the morning though you have no power to control what happens to you in your sleep. How do I know you have faith in waking up...because you made plans for tomorrow. See, you have more faith than you think. The problem is you are not lining your faith up in the right direction. Since you are already operating by God's principles, why not just give the guy a try and use the same principles for creating the steps leading to your success.

You have more power than you give yourself credit for. Nothing can stop you except you. Prayer sets the tone for everything. Prayer is the unfair advantage that we all have access to and when applied correctly, with the right amount of faith, there is no limitation available that can stop you from becoming whatever it is you have a desire to become. Trust the process. Believe that your words have authority. Believe that God created you to be great and not mediocre. You are not designed to be insignificant, but instead you are born to be a trailblazer. Life can truly be as we 'call it'. We just have to trust that the words we call have enough power to create what only our minds can see. For those that say they have to see it to believe it, I say fine. Then close your eyes, take a strong deep breath, repeat that breath, and get quiet for approximately one minute. Now, the very thing you say you need to see in order to believe, I suggest you 'see it' now while your eyes are closed. Create the actual image that you want to see exactly the way you need to see it. Watch it for as long as you can stand before opening your eyes. Now that we got that out the way, let's get to it since

you were able to just see it to believe it.

CHAPTER 9

STAY READY

I have a really good friend from college who spent most of his life playing football. It was a sport he was extremely passionate about and even though he didn't play for the team in college he still found a way to stay around the sport by enjoying intramural football. One day while still an undergrad, he decided to tryout for the cheerleading squad. His initial reasoning, as most college guys would suggest, was to be closely connected to the female cheerleaders as would probably be most guys dream. However, he became very involved with the sport and fell in love with it.

In fact, he loved cheerleading so much that even after college he joined a professional cheerleading organization to stay around the fire and be involved. During this time, although he was engaged in cheerleading on the side, he found a career in a totally different arena under law enforcement. However, his passion for the sport never died. One day he traveled up to Baltimore. I believe this was a vacation he'd taken from work to enjoy a football game in which he may have been invited to by a friend who was a cheerleader for the NFL team there. He had great seats which were close to the cheerleaders so that he could see not only the game but watch them as well. Keep in mind, he never lost his passion and he continued to deal with cheerleading outside of college up until this point. What ends up transpiring is nothing shy of amazing and what many would say, "That was all God." Here it is, he is enjoying the football game and appreciating the moment of being there. Then suddenly his friend calls him down to the spot where the cheerleaders where located. It turns out that one of the male cheerleaders was dealing with an injury and they needed a replacement at that moment! Because he was still active in his dream passion, which secretly was a career he badly wanted, he was readily available when the time finally came. Fast forward to now, he is a full-time cheerleader and personal trainer in Baltimore living his dream eight years later. Why is this story important? Many times, we get so caught in the "right now" of life we tend to forget that our heart's desire could manifest itself at any given moment. The bottom line is if you stay ready, you don't have to get ready. How many times have we heard that statement? I'm sure a million times before today and it is very true yet and still.

The moment you make up your mind as to what you want to do or accomplish in life, your spirit and energy sets the tone for what comes your way. Sometimes, it could be as fast as my friend's opportunity was with cheerleading and you could be called to your passion and purpose at the spare of a moment. Then there are times when it could take years, or even decades, before your desire manifests itself. Either way, you do not want the story to go, "I could have been a very successful blah blah but I wasn't ready when the time came." (Insert sad face here). The one thing I know for a fact is that time waits for no man. Even though I have to "secure the bag" doing things that may be outside of my true passion, I never cease to stay involved with the things that line me up with what my heart desires. I do not shy away from going to events and functions where I could meet individuals who may be doing exceptionally well whom I could learn from. I take time, even if only an hour a week, to watch videos and learn more about how to be efficient with creating goals that could get me a step closer to where I would like to be. I find people to shadow that are winning on a high level that I can imitate (if it ain't broke, don't fix it) so that I too can create a level of success for myself. And this isn't only when dealing with my dream or passion but in EVERYTHING that I do I look to see who is doing it better and how I can mimic what they are doing. And as you begin to do this, you will notice that each level you climb there will be one more person a step higher to follow. And what do you do? Can you guess it? That's right. The same procedure as before. You mimic what they are doing until you master the craft.

The key is to always be working on yourself and your skill set. Never let a moment go by that you ignore the opportunity to get better than you were a day ago. Never take a day, a moment, or a second for granted because the opportunity doesn't stop at you just because you are where it started. As the saying goes, "next man up". And the last thing you ever want to do is find yourself ready later than you should have been and playing catch up to who you should have been ahead.

One of the most devastating actions that a person can partake that is the single most killer of 'being ready for the moment' is procrastination! I see it so much with individuals that are just starting in business or a task deemed as important to them yet their actions say otherwise. One of the things about procrastination is that it gives a nasty stigma about you that says you can't be trusted (mainly associated with important deadlines or simply being the go to guy for a time sensitive project), you're not mature enough, or you just don't take the business/assignment/project seriously. It's amazing how no one really pays attention to the fact that time management is so important that it's even documented how often you were late in middle and high school. If you were pull up your old high school records today, a person can see how often you made it to school tardy and it was more so your parents fault at that point in life, yet it is still documented. Isn't that something? People have lost jobs from simply procrastinating on getting their work attire prepared in a timely manner causing them to be late for work too many times leading to termination. Now why would you risk losing money simply from procrastinating? Men and women have shown up late for seminars that were time sensitive and not being allowed inside when the information given would have propelled their business or intellect in a certain skill set that could have created a huge financial boost in their product or business. I've seen people simply practice procrastination to the point they are late to their children's graduation and completely missed them walking the stage and receiving their diploma or degree. When others see that you are habitual at being late or indulge heavily in procrastinating with everything that you do, they don't take you or whatever it is you are doing as serious and then you miss out on a potential partner, customer, client, or supporter. No one wants to stamp their name on someone or something that's questionable and being late all the time gives that vibe.

Being ready simply means doing all you can, as best you can, as much as you can to be available to move forward when your name is called. You may not be completely equipped with all you need at that time, but you don't have to worry about providing an excuse to not be present in the moment. Sometimes just simply being ready and/or being available is the only step you need to advance to the next level because you never know what or who is on the other side waiting for you to walk through the door. Don't spend too much time overthinking or sleeping on your opportunity. Keep moving, keep learning, keep pushing, keep applying, keep running, and don't quit. Just simply be dressed and when it's time to leave, all you should have to do is just put on your shoes. Now let's get it!

CHAPTER 10

IN CLOSING

What you have just read are some of the basic ideas and behaviors that I have studied over the years that I have applied to my own life. I am a firm believer that in all things, no matter how farfetched they may sound, we are more than capable to accomplish our goals and dreams. Staying ready is a process. There are steps that you must take first to get ready, and then you must take more steps to stay ready so that when your name is called you can go right in as though you were always there.

I believe that everyone has their "season". At some point, if you keep working at something long enough and hard enough, you will definitely reap the benefits of the effort you have sown. In some shape, form, or fashion you will find yourself in position for the very thing you have fought for. Don't get used to looking at the clock. Some people don't lose any time and can just go right into what their hearts desire with no pressure, trouble, or distractions getting in their way. Then there are those who have to go the length of time, it seems, and conquer a million barriers before getting to the other side. It does not matter which part of the equation you find yourself. All that matters is that you make it to the finish line. Focus only on what you can control and ignore what you can't change. I will say that again in case you nodded off on that part. Focus only on what you can control and ignore what you can't change. Things will happen. Keep going. Distractions may arise. Keep going. Heartache may show up. Keep going. Pain may set in. Keep going. People you love may leave. Keep going. Those that you trust may turn on you. Keep going. You may bleed and sweat a little more than you wish. Keep going. Your name may get bashed and ridiculed. Keep going. You may lose sleep many nights. Keep going. You may miss a few meals and family functions. Keep going. People you love might start talking negatively about you. Keep going. You may fall more times than you can count. Keep going. You may lose a car or two or get evicted. Keep going. You may find yourself asking for help or to borrow money to get by. Keep going. You may cry out to God and hear no reply. Keep going. No matter what the situation. No matter how bad it gets. No matter how much pressure you are under. The only thing you can control is your desire to keep going. So I say to you on today that you are a victor, you are a conqueror, you are superior and not inferior, and most importantly, you can and WILL keep going! I'm Rod Shipp and I keep going!

ABOUT THE AUTHOR

Rod Shipp is a native of Memphis, TN and grew up in the Binghampton community where he developed a passion for writing through poetry when he was 10 years old. He was an excellent student, who was in the honors program, as well as an amazing athlete participating in football and track. He has been known by many of his peers to be one of the most hardworking, dedicated people you would ever meet. Hardly ever backing down from any challenge whatsoever.

In his college years, he majored in Health and Human Performance as he had an interest in personal training, which is something he maintained for about 10 years. He wrote his first book in college entitled "My Loud Silence" which was a compilation of poetry he had written dating back to his middle school years. He never published the book but a few of those poems made there way to his next book "Rain From a Cloudless Sky" which he did publish and is available along with his first novel "Scent of a Kiss" on www.lulu.com.

Today, Rod is a successful business owner and entrepreneur and has his sights set on becoming a fulltime investor over the course of the next 5 years or sooner. He loves giving back to those who are less fortunate and spends a great deal of time encouraging and motivating those around him to strive higher and fight harder to achieve their dreams. In short, he is an amazing human being who is ready to take on the world to achieve more.

ACKNOWLEDGEMENTS

What can I say? These last few years have been quite the journey to say the least. Through many hardships, severe trials, and disastrous errors, I have made it. I am here right now smiling from ear to ear because what I went through didn't take me out. I couldn't have done that without a strong group of individuals behind me to encourage me to continue my fight. There are way too many names to list and I don't want to make anyone mad but there are some names I just ABSOLUTELY cannot leave out. But for those who know you were there and don't see your name here, just know I haven't forgotten you and, Lord willing, I will be certain to mention you all in the next book. But I have to start with the ones who saw that stayed out of trouble these past 3 years and they know why but Steven "Polo" McRae, TJ Beattie, Howard "Squirt" Branch III, and Jeffrey Higgins III have been my crutch preventing failure these last few years. My godmothers Gwen Redmond and Melissa

Bishop and my godfather Roy Bishop have been my safe haven. My mother Tammy Bowles, my aunts Reeshemah Joy Burrow and Tersa "Tolly" Jones have always been a call away. My friends who are like brothers and sisters that keep me in check are (in no particular order) Michael Fields Jr, Venisha Brooks, Tara Schukert, David Jordan Jr, Galen Jones, Kenny Sipp, Cheyanne Patterson, Pam Joyner-Robinson, Tequilla Calhoun, Albert and Natasha Miles, Jonathan Pierce, Michael Peters, Anthony "TJ" Joseph, and Nolyn Johnson Jr. Please trust there are many others I could name but this is just in reference to the last few years which are vital to today. I have a couple of cousins to mention as Tricha King and Jerome Jackson were definitely there for me during some tough times. And my brother Courtney Williams and sisters Allyson Shipp, Laquisa Alexander, and Kandy Burks all have a huge place to call home in my heart. And lastly, but not least, My Pastor and brother in law, Corey Alexander for always being a call away when I needed him the most. Thank yall! Thank yall! Thank yall from the depths of my heart! I mean it! Until next time, peace and blessings! Shipp…

Peace and Blessings…Shipp